VEHICLE INFORMATION

Make:_____ Model:_____

Year:_____ License Plate:_____

VIN:_____

Purchase Date:_____ From:_____ _____

Dealer Info:_____ _____

Registration:_____ _____

_____ _____

Insurance Company:_____ _____ _____

Agent:_____ _____

Phone:_____

Policy:_____

Notes:_____

_____

_____

Date/Time	Oil Changed	Rotate/Balance Tires	Tire Replaced	Wheel Alignment	Air Filter	Fuel Filter	Brakes Serviced	Spark Plugs	Transmission	Wiper Blades	Batteries	Radiator	Belts & Hoses	Mileage

OTHER MAINTENANCE / REPAIRS LOG

Date/Time	Description	Mileage

Date/Time	Oil Changed	Rotate/Balance Tires	Tire Replaced	Wheel Alignment	Air Filter	Fuel Filter	Brakes Serviced	Spark Plugs	Transmission	Wiper Blades	Batteries	Radiator	Belts & Hoses	Mileage

OTHER MAINTENANCE / REPAIRS LOG

Date/Time	Description	Mileage

Date/Time	Oil Changed	Rotate/Balance Tires	Tire Replaced	Wheel Alignment	Air Filter	Fuel Filter	Brakes Serviced	Spark Plugs	Transmission	Wiper Blades	Batteries	Radiator	Belts & Hoses	Mileage

OTHER MAINTENANCE / REPAIRS LOG

Date/Time	Description	Mileage

Date/Time	Oil Changed	Rotate/Balance Tires	Tire Replaced	Wheel Alignment	Air Filter	Fuel Filter	Brakes Serviced	Spark Plugs	Transmission	Wiper Blades	Batteries	Radiator	Belts & Hoses	Mileage

OTHER MAINTENANCE / REPAIRS LOG

Date/Time	Description	Mileage

📅 Date/Time	Oil Changed	Rotate/Balance Tires	Tire Replaced	Wheel Alignment	Air Filter	Fuel Filter	Brakes Serviced	Spark Plugs	Transmission	Wiper Blades	Batteries	Radiator	Belts & Hoses	🕐 Mileage

OTHER MAINTENANCE / REPAIRS LOG

Date/Time	Description	Mileage

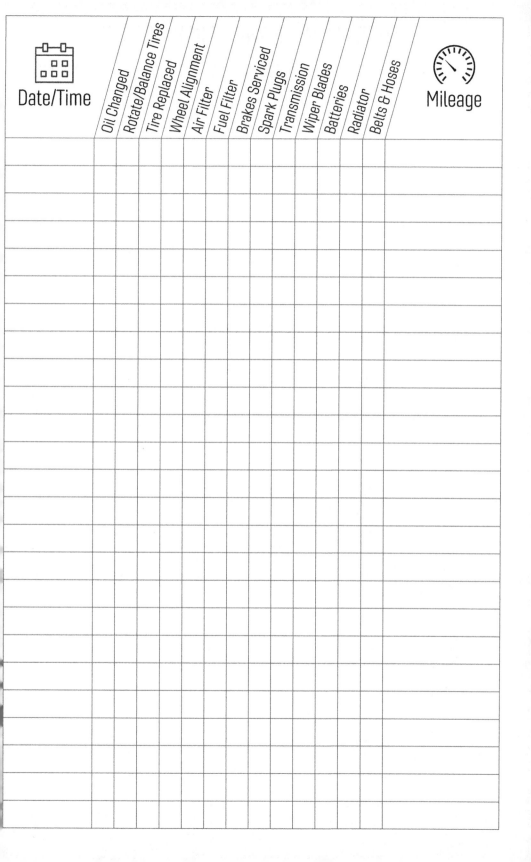

Date/Time	Oil Changed	Rotate/Balance Tires	Tire Replaced	Wheel Alignment	Air Filter	Fuel Filter	Brakes Serviced	Spark Plugs	Transmission	Wiper Blades	Batteries	Radiator	Belts & Hoses	Mileage

OTHER MAINTENANCE / REPAIRS LOG

Date/Time	Description	Mileage

Date/Time	Oil Changed	Rotate/Balance Tires	Tire Replaced	Wheel Alignment	Air Filter	Fuel Filter	Brakes Serviced	Spark Plugs	Transmission	Wiper Blades	Batteries	Radiator	Belts & Hoses	Mileage

OTHER MAINTENANCE / REPAIRS LOG

Date/Time	Description	Mileage

Date/Time	Oil Changed	Rotate/Balance Tires	Tire Replaced	Wheel Alignment	Air Filter	Fuel Filter	Brakes Serviced	Spark Plugs	Transmission	Wiper Blades	Batteries	Radiator	Belts & Hoses	Mileage

OTHER MAINTENANCE / REPAIRS LOG

Date/Time	Description	Mileage

Date/Time	Oil Changed	Rotate/Balance Tires	Tire Replaced	Wheel Alignment	Air Filter	Fuel Filter	Brakes Serviced	Spark Plugs	Transmission	Wiper Blades	Batteries	Radiator	Belts & Hoses	Mileage

OTHER MAINTENANCE / REPAIRS LOG

Date/Time	Description	Mileage

Date/Time	Oil Changed	Rotate/Balance Tires	Tire Replaced	Wheel Alignment	Air Filter	Fuel Filter	Brakes Serviced	Spark Plugs	Transmission	Wiper Blades	Batteries	Radiator	Belts & Hoses	Mileage

OTHER MAINTENANCE / REPAIRS LOG

Date/Time	Description	Mileage

Date/Time	Oil Changed	Rotate/Balance Tires	Tire Replaced	Wheel Alignment	Air Filter	Fuel Filter	Brakes Serviced	Spark Plugs	Transmission	Wiper Blades	Batteries	Radiator	Belts & Hoses	Mileage

OTHER MAINTENANCE / REPAIRS LOG

Date/Time	Description	Mileage

Date/Time	Oil Changed	Rotate/Balance Tires	Tire Replaced	Wheel Alignment	Air Filter	Fuel Filter	Brakes Serviced	Spark Plugs	Transmission	Wiper Blades	Batteries	Radiator	Belts & Hoses	Mileage

OTHER MAINTENANCE / REPAIRS LOG

Date/Time	Description	Mileage

Date/Time	Oil Changed	Rotate/Balance Tires	Tire Replaced	Wheel Alignment	Air Filter	Fuel Filter	Brakes Serviced	Spark Plugs	Transmission	Wiper Blades	Batteries	Radiator	Belts & Hoses	Mileage

OTHER MAINTENANCE / REPAIRS LOG

Date/Time	Description	Mileage

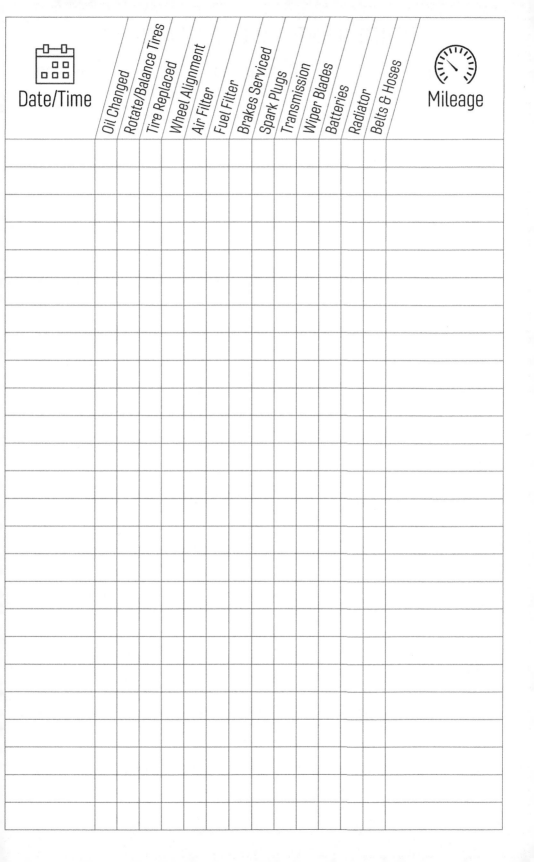

Date/Time	Oil Changed	Rotate/Balance Tires	Tire Replaced	Wheel Alignment	Air Filter	Fuel Filter	Brakes Serviced	Spark Plugs	Transmission	Wiper Blades	Batteries	Radiator	Belts & Hoses	Mileage

OTHER MAINTENANCE / REPAIRS LOG

Date/Time	Description	Mileage

Date/Time	Oil Changed	Rotate/Balance Tires	Tire Replaced	Wheel Alignment	Air Filter	Fuel Filter	Brakes Serviced	Spark Plugs	Transmission	Wiper Blades	Batteries	Radiator	Belts & Hoses	Mileage

OTHER MAINTENANCE / REPAIRS LOG

Date/Time	Description	Mileage

Date/Time	Oil Changed	Rotate/Balance Tires	Tire Replaced	Wheel Alignment	Air Filter	Fuel Filter	Brakes Serviced	Spark Plugs	Transmission	Wiper Blades	Batteries	Radiator	Belts & Hoses	Mileage

OTHER MAINTENANCE / REPAIRS LOG

Date/Time	Description	Mileage

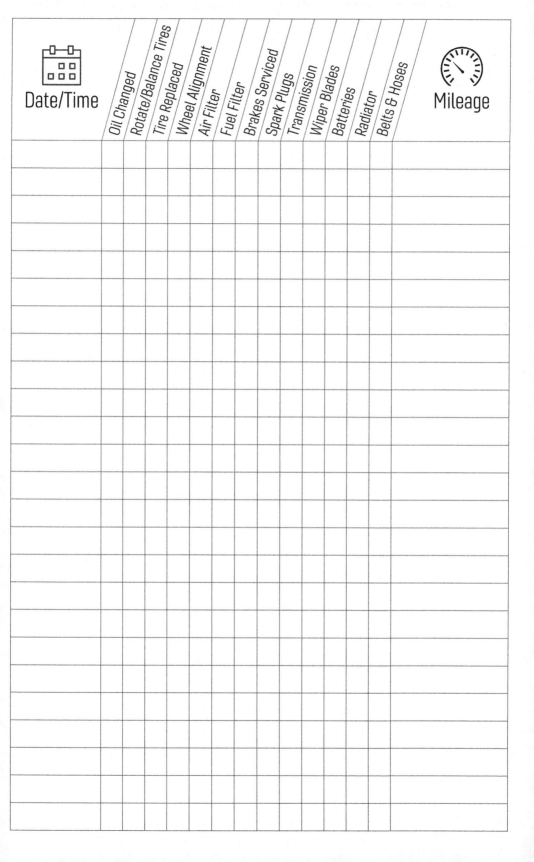

Date/Time	Oil Changed	Rotate/Balance Tires	Tire Replaced	Wheel Alignment	Air Filter	Fuel Filter	Brakes Serviced	Spark Plugs	Transmission	Wiper Blades	Batteries	Radiator	Belts & Hoses	Mileage

OTHER MAINTENANCE / REPAIRS LOG

Date/Time	Description	Mileage

Date/Time	Oil Changed	Rotate/Balance Tires	Tire Replaced	Wheel Alignment	Air Filter	Fuel Filter	Brakes Serviced	Spark Plugs	Transmission	Wiper Blades	Batteries	Radiator	Belts & Hoses	Mileage

OTHER MAINTENANCE / REPAIRS LOG

Date/Time	Description	Mileage

Date/Time	Oil Changed	Rotate/Balance Tires	Tire Replaced	Wheel Alignment	Air Filter	Fuel Filter	Brakes Serviced	Spark Plugs	Transmission	Wiper Blades	Batteries	Radiator	Belts & Hoses	Mileage

OTHER MAINTENANCE / REPAIRS LOG

Date/Time	Description	Mileage

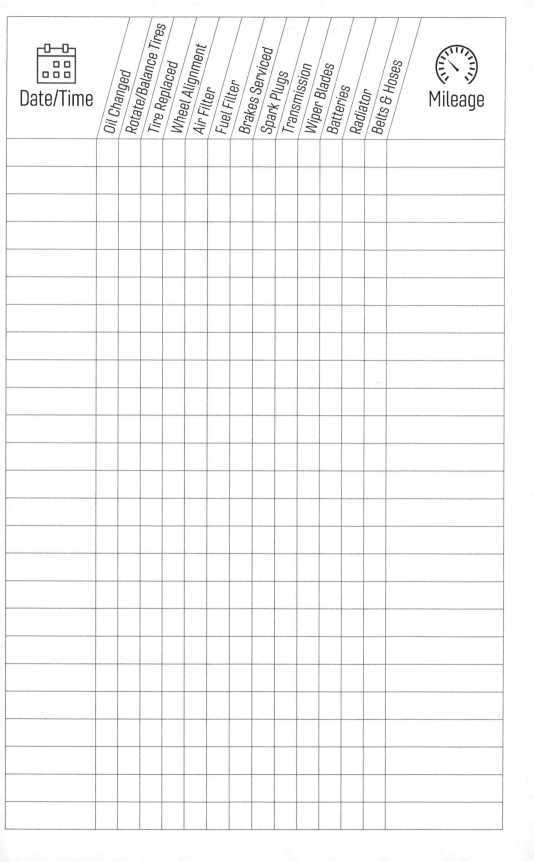

Date/Time	Oil Changed	Rotate/Balance Tires	Tire Replaced	Wheel Alignment	Air Filter	Fuel Filter	Brakes Serviced	Spark Plugs	Transmission	Wiper Blades	Batteries	Radiator	Belts & Hoses	Mileage

OTHER MAINTENANCE / REPAIRS LOG

Date/Time	Description	Mileage

Date/Time	Oil Changed	Rotate/Balance Tires	Tire Replaced	Wheel Alignment	Air Filter	Fuel Filter	Brakes Serviced	Spark Plugs	Transmission	Wiper Blades	Batteries	Radiator	Belts & Hoses	Mileage

OTHER MAINTENANCE / REPAIRS LOG

Date/Time	Description	Mileage

Date/Time	Oil Changed	Rotate/Balance Tires	Tire Replaced	Wheel Alignment	Air Filter	Fuel Filter	Brakes Serviced	Spark Plugs	Transmission	Wiper Blades	Batteries	Radiator	Belts & Hoses	Mileage

OTHER MAINTENANCE / REPAIRS LOG

Date/Time	Description	Mileage

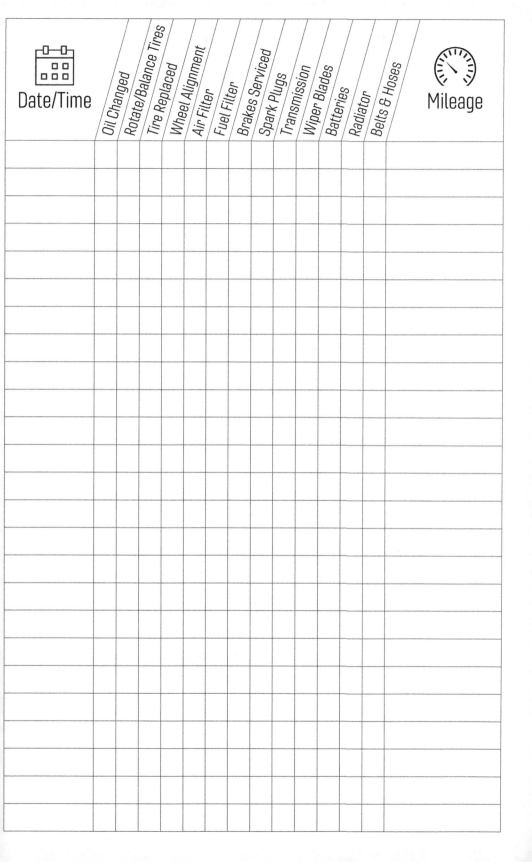

Date/Time	Oil Changed	Rotate/Balance Tires	Tire Replaced	Wheel Alignment	Air Filter	Fuel Filter	Brakes Serviced	Spark Plugs	Transmission	Wiper Blades	Batteries	Radiator	Belts & Hoses	Mileage

OTHER MAINTENANCE / REPAIRS LOG

Date/Time	Description	Mileage

Date/Time	Oil Changed	Rotate/Balance Tires	Tire Replaced	Wheel Alignment	Air Filter	Fuel Filter	Brakes Serviced	Spark Plugs	Transmission	Wiper Blades	Batteries	Radiator	Belts & Hoses	Mileage

OTHER MAINTENANCE / REPAIRS LOG

Date/Time	Description	Mileage

Date/Time	Oil Changed	Rotate/Balance Tires	Tire Replaced	Wheel Alignment	Air Filter	Fuel Filter	Brakes Serviced	Spark Plugs	Transmission	Wiper Blades	Batteries	Radiator	Belts & Hoses	Mileage

OTHER MAINTENANCE / REPAIRS LOG

Date/Time	Description	Mileage

Date/Time	Oil Changed	Rotate/Balance Tires	Tire Replaced	Wheel Alignment	Air Filter	Fuel Filter	Brakes Serviced	Spark Plugs	Transmission	Wiper Blades	Batteries	Radiator	Belts & Hoses	Mileage

OTHER MAINTENANCE / REPAIRS LOG

Date/Time	Description	Mileage

Date/Time	Oil Changed	Rotate/Balance Tires	Tire Replaced	Wheel Alignment	Air Filter	Fuel Filter	Brakes Serviced	Spark Plugs	Transmission	Wiper Blades	Batteries	Radiator	Belts & Hoses	Mileage

OTHER MAINTENANCE / REPAIRS LOG

Date/Time	Description	Mileage

Date/Time	Oil Changed	Rotate/Balance Tires	Tire Replaced	Wheel Alignment	Air Filter	Fuel Filter	Brakes Serviced	Spark Plugs	Transmission	Wiper Blades	Batteries	Radiator	Belts & Hoses	Mileage

OTHER MAINTENANCE / REPAIRS LOG

Date/Time	Description	Mileage

Date/Time	Oil Changed	Rotate/Balance Tires	Tire Replaced	Wheel Alignment	Air Filter	Fuel Filter	Brakes Serviced	Spark Plugs	Transmission	Wiper Blades	Batteries	Radiator	Belts & Hoses	Mileage

OTHER MAINTENANCE / REPAIRS LOG

Date/Time	Description	Mileage

Date/Time	Oil Changed	Rotate/Balance Tires	Tire Replaced	Wheel Alignment	Air Filter	Fuel Filter	Brakes Serviced	Spark Plugs	Transmission	Wiper Blades	Batteries	Radiator	Belts & Hoses	Mileage

OTHER MAINTENANCE / REPAIRS LOG

Date/Time	Description	Mileage

Date/Time	Oil Changed	Rotate/Balance Tires	Tire Replaced	Wheel Alignment	Air Filter	Fuel Filter	Brakes Serviced	Spark Plugs	Transmission	Wiper Blades	Batteries	Radiator	Belts & Hoses	Mileage

OTHER MAINTENANCE / REPAIRS LOG

Date/Time	Description	Mileage

Date/Time	Oil Changed	Rotate/Balance Tires	Tire Replaced	Wheel Alignment	Air Filter	Fuel Filter	Brakes Serviced	Spark Plugs	Transmission	Wiper Blades	Batteries	Radiator	Belts & Hoses	Mileage

OTHER MAINTENANCE / REPAIRS LOG

Date/Time	Description	Mileage

Date/Time	Oil Changed	Rotate/Balance Tires	Tire Replaced	Wheel Alignment	Air Filter	Fuel Filter	Brakes Serviced	Spark Plugs	Transmission	Wiper Blades	Batteries	Radiator	Belts & Hoses	Mileage

OTHER MAINTENANCE / REPAIRS LOG

Date/Time	Description	Mileage

Date/Time	Oil Changed	Rotate/Balance Tires	Tire Replaced	Wheel Alignment	Air Filter	Fuel Filter	Brakes Serviced	Spark Plugs	Transmission	Wiper Blades	Batteries	Radiator	Belts & Hoses	Mileage

OTHER MAINTENANCE / REPAIRS LOG		
Date/Time	Description	Mileage

Date/Time	Oil Changed	Rotate/Balance Tires	Tire Replaced	Wheel Alignment	Air Filter	Fuel Filter	Brakes Serviced	Spark Plugs	Transmission	Wiper Blades	Batteries	Radiator	Belts & Hoses	Mileage

OTHER MAINTENANCE / REPAIRS LOG

Date/Time	Description	Mileage

Date/Time	Oil Changed	Rotate/Balance Tires	Tire Replaced	Wheel Alignment	Air Filter	Fuel Filter	Brakes Serviced	Spark Plugs	Transmission	Wiper Blades	Batteries	Radiator	Belts & Hoses	Mileage

OTHER MAINTENANCE / REPAIRS LOG

Date/Time	Description	Mileage

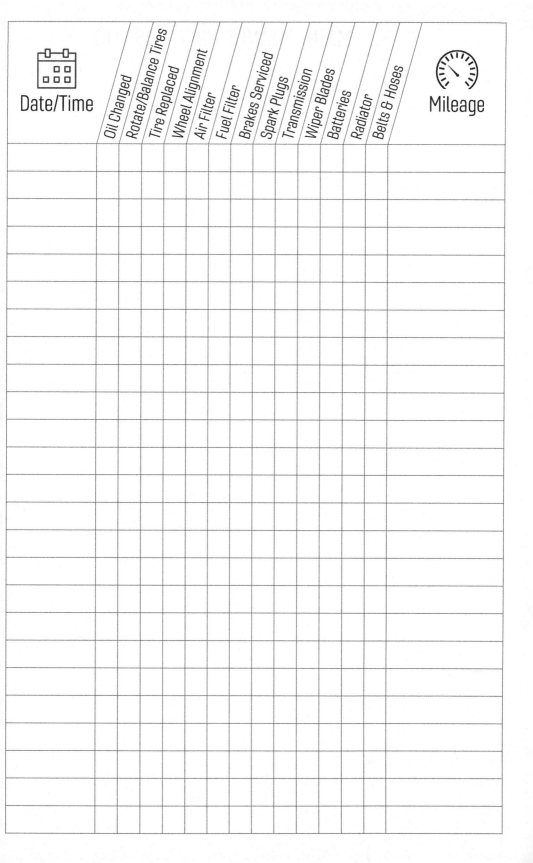

Date/Time	Oil Changed	Rotate/Balance Tires	Tire Replaced	Wheel Alignment	Air Filter	Fuel Filter	Brakes Serviced	Spark Plugs	Transmission	Wiper Blades	Batteries	Radiator	Belts & Hoses	Mileage

OTHER MAINTENANCE / REPAIRS LOG

Date/Time	Description	Mileage

Date/Time	Oil Changed	Rotate/Balance Tires	Tire Replaced	Wheel Alignment	Air Filter	Fuel Filter	Brakes Serviced	Spark Plugs	Transmission	Wiper Blades	Batteries	Radiator	Belts & Hoses	Mileage

OTHER MAINTENANCE / REPAIRS LOG

Date/Time	Description	Mileage

Date/Time	Oil Changed	Rotate/Balance Tires	Tire Replaced	Wheel Alignment	Air Filter	Fuel Filter	Brakes Serviced	Spark Plugs	Transmission	Wiper Blades	Batteries	Radiator	Belts & Hoses	Mileage

OTHER MAINTENANCE / REPAIRS LOG

Date/Time	Description	Mileage

Date/Time	Oil Changed	Rotate/Balance Tires	Tire Replaced	Wheel Alignment	Air Filter	Fuel Filter	Brakes Serviced	Spark Plugs	Transmission	Wiper Blades	Batteries	Radiator	Belts & Hoses	Mileage

OTHER MAINTENANCE / REPAIRS LOG

Date/Time	Description	Mileage

Date/Time	Oil Changed	Rotate/Balance Tires	Tire Replaced	Wheel Alignment	Air Filter	Fuel Filter	Brakes Serviced	Spark Plugs	Transmission	Wiper Blades	Batteries	Radiator	Belts & Hoses	Mileage

OTHER MAINTENANCE / REPAIRS LOG

Date/Time	Description	Mileage

Date/Time	Oil Changed	Rotate/Balance Tires	Tire Replaced	Wheel Alignment	Air Filter	Fuel Filter	Brakes Serviced	Spark Plugs	Transmission	Wiper Blades	Batteries	Radiator	Belts & Hoses	Mileage

OTHER MAINTENANCE / REPAIRS LOG

Date/Time	Description	Mileage

Date/Time	Oil Changed	Rotate/Balance Tires	Tire Replaced	Wheel Alignment	Air Filter	Fuel Filter	Brakes Serviced	Spark Plugs	Transmission	Wiper Blades	Batteries	Radiator	Belts & Hoses	Mileage

OTHER MAINTENANCE / REPAIRS LOG

Date/Time	Description	Mileage

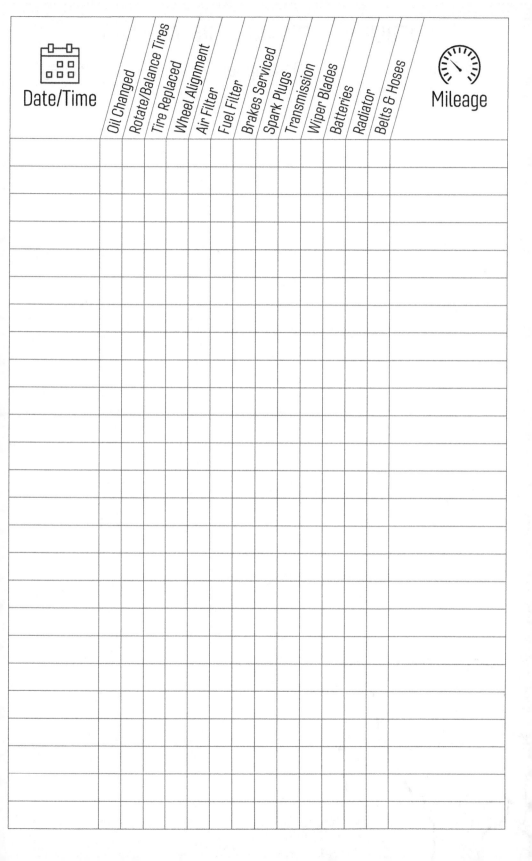

Date/Time	Oil Changed	Rotate/Balance Tires	Tire Replaced	Wheel Alignment	Air Filter	Fuel Filter	Brakes Serviced	Spark Plugs	Transmission	Wiper Blades	Batteries	Radiator	Belts & Hoses	Mileage

OTHER MAINTENANCE / REPAIRS LOG

Date/Time	Description	Mileage

Date/Time	Oil Changed	Rotate/Balance Tires	Tire Replaced	Wheel Alignment	Air Filter	Fuel Filter	Brakes Serviced	Spark Plugs	Transmission	Wiper Blades	Batteries	Radiator	Belts & Hoses	Mileage

OTHER MAINTENANCE / REPAIRS LOG

Date/Time	Description	Mileage

Date/Time	Oil Changed	Rotate/Balance Tires	Tire Replaced	Wheel Alignment	Air Filter	Fuel Filter	Brakes Serviced	Spark Plugs	Transmission	Wiper Blades	Batteries	Radiator	Belts & Hoses	Mileage

OTHER MAINTENANCE / REPAIRS LOG

Date/Time	Description	Mileage

Date/Time	Oil Changed	Rotate/Balance Tires	Tire Replaced	Wheel Alignment	Air Filter	Fuel Filter	Brakes Serviced	Spark Plugs	Transmission	Wiper Blades	Batteries	Radiator	Belts & Hoses	Mileage

OTHER MAINTENANCE / REPAIRS LOG

Date/Time	Description	Mileage

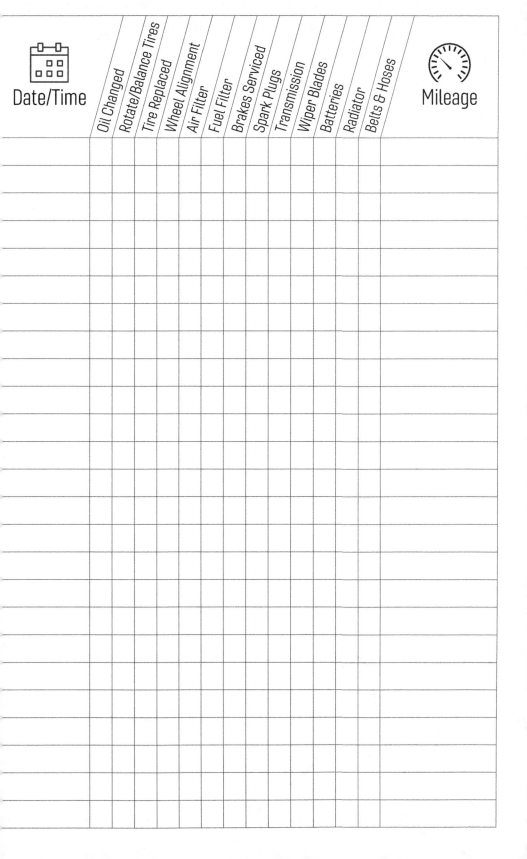

Date/Time	Oil Changed	Rotate/Balance Tires	Tire Replaced	Wheel Alignment	Air Filter	Fuel Filter	Brakes Serviced	Spark Plugs	Transmission	Wiper Blades	Batteries	Radiator	Belts & Hoses	Mileage

OTHER MAINTENANCE / REPAIRS LOG

Date/Time	Description	Mileage

Date/Time	Oil Changed	Rotate/Balance Tires	Tire Replaced	Wheel Alignment	Air Filter	Fuel Filter	Brakes Serviced	Spark Plugs	Transmission	Wiper Blades	Batteries	Radiator	Belts & Hoses	Mileage

OTHER MAINTENANCE / REPAIRS LOG

Date/Time	Description	Mileage

Date/Time	Oil Changed	Rotate/Balance Tires	Tire Replaced	Wheel Alignment	Air Filter	Fuel Filter	Brakes Serviced	Spark Plugs	Transmission	Wiper Blades	Batteries	Radiator	Belts & Hoses	Mileage

OTHER MAINTENANCE / REPAIRS LOG

Date/Time	Description	Mileage

Date/Time	Oil Changed	Rotate/Balance Tires	Tire Replaced	Wheel Alignment	Air Filter	Fuel Filter	Brakes Serviced	Spark Plugs	Transmission	Wiper Blades	Batteries	Radiator	Belts & Hoses	Mileage

OTHER MAINTENANCE / REPAIRS LOG

Date/Time	Description	Mileage

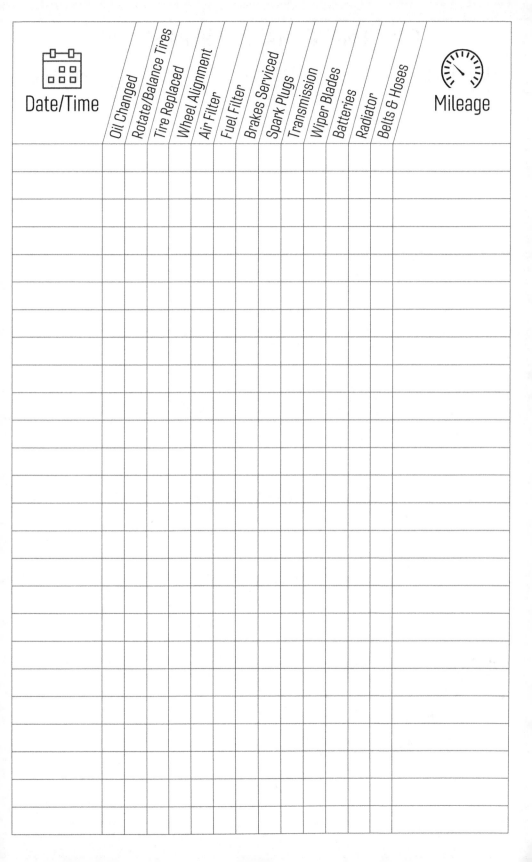

Date/Time	Oil Changed	Rotate/Balance Tires	Tire Replaced	Wheel Alignment	Air Filter	Fuel Filter	Brakes Serviced	Spark Plugs	Transmission	Wiper Blades	Batteries	Radiator	Belts & Hoses	Mileage

OTHER MAINTENANCE / REPAIRS LOG

Date/Time	Description	Mileage

Date/Time	Oil Changed	Rotate/Balance Tires	Tire Replaced	Wheel Alignment	Air Filter	Fuel Filter	Brakes Serviced	Spark Plugs	Transmission	Wiper Blades	Batteries	Radiator	Belts & Hoses	Mileage

OTHER MAINTENANCE / REPAIRS LOG

Date/Time	Description	Mileage

Date/Time	Oil Changed	Rotate/Balance Tires	Tire Replaced	Wheel Alignment	Air Filter	Fuel Filter	Brakes Serviced	Spark Plugs	Transmission	Wiper Blades	Batteries	Radiator	Belts & Hoses	Mileage

OTHER MAINTENANCE / REPAIRS LOG

Date/Time	Description	Mileage

Made in the USA
Middletown, DE
15 July 2023

35248617R00066